Also by Michael Bernard Beckwith

*Spiritual Liberation*
*Fulfilling Your Soul's Potential*

*40-Day Mind Fast Soul Feast*

*Inspirations of the Heart*

*A Manifesto of Peace*

*Living from the Overflow*

# THE ANSWER IS YOU

## MICHAEL BERNARD BECKWITH

Edited by Anita Rehker

Agape Media International
Los Angeles, California

**Agape Media International, LLC**
5700 Buckingham Parkway
Culver City, California 90230
310-348-1260, Ext 1601
www.agapemedia-international.com

*The Answer Is You*
Michael Bernard Beckwith

Editor: Anita Rehker
Cover Photo: Mikki Willis
Cover Design: Brooks Cole
Interior Design: Trish Weber Hall
Typography: Craig Woods, Donalyn Brooks Catalano
Transcriptions: Christina Migliorino
Publication Executive: Stephen Powers

Published by Agape Media International, LLC.
Printed in USA on recycled paper

ISBN13:   978-0-9700327-5-7

Based on the PBS Television Special
*The Answer Is You*
Michael Bernard Beckwith

Special thanks to
Agape International Spiritual Center
www.agapelive.com

*To my beloved family members who grace my life with their loving hearts, and to my global spiritual family of students with whom I have the honor and privilege of sharing the journey of spiritual awakening.*

# CONTENTS

# AUTHOR'S NOTE

The human yearning to connect with something of cosmic significance has birthed the world's philosophical schools, scientific communities, and spiritual traditions, which have for millennia questioned and explored the origins and meaning of existence.

Our spirit of creative inquiry begins very early on. Just ask parents and they will verify that the mantra most devotedly practiced by their young children consists of one word: "Why?" A father of two myself, as my son and daughter outgrew the "Why" stage, their adolescent inquiries aimed at a most sensitive target: the questioning of parental authority itself. Their in-your-face directness urged me to question my own authoritative sources which eventually led me to expand the African proverb, "It takes a village to raise a child" to include "….likewise, it takes a child to raise a village."

But questioning is not only the domain of the young. Once activated, the innate impulse to question simply does not go away. At every age and stage of development questions energize our thinking and expand our awareness. For example, people of all ages, races, and cultures claim that they have experienced spontaneous healings, answered prayer, beatific visions and other phenomena that are not backed up by empirical evidence. According to a 2007 Harris Poll, four out of five individuals believe miracles are real, and nearly two-thirds personally know someone who has experienced one. Are such experiences genuine? Are they all in one's head? "There are only two ways to live your life," Albert Einstein extolled, "one is as though nothing is a miracle. The other is as if everything is. I believe in the latter."

Questioning our tidy answers, cherished beliefs, and the authoritative sources that have influenced our values and creeds for living leads us on a pathway to deeper self-discovery. Asking creates space for new realties to enter our experience; it invites us into perceptions larger than our unexamined reference points. Questioning is not a lack of faith; it inspires us to grow beyond faith into trust. What have you recently changed your mind about or shifted your point of view on through the process of questioning?

It's very encouraging how the simple act of questioning offers us a completely different perspective on who we are and what our role is in the creation of our life. Big questions place us right on the dot: If the universe is governed by natural laws, then what is their source, and what is their purpose in human life? Are we central to the universe? If so, what does that mean for us? Does holistic thinking offer us a more accurate worldview? Are individuals who believe they have the answers happier than those who continue to question?

Questions are a celebration of human inquiry. Consider the Buddhist koan, which is meant to provide thought-tools to bring about a deeper awareness of reality. A frequently quoted koan is, "What did your face look like before your parents were born?" Such paradoxical queries send us on a quest for spiritual and philosophical integrity. Torah commentator Iba Ezra said, "One who is ashamed to ask will diminish wisdom among men."

The act of questioning can be a vulnerable experience. Taking action on the answers to our questions may result in our being ostracized by our family or social group if we abandon their accepted belief system. There are risks, yes, but the rewards are life-transforming. As human beings, every day we are faced with questions from small to great that inform our decision-making and life choices. The resulting actions we take impact not only ourselves, they also affect those in our immediate sphere of influence and ultimately our world.

When I teach on this subject it's not uncommon for someone to ask, "Is there a hierarchy of questioning in that some questions are of more benefit than others?" Experience has convinced me that while there definitely are no wrong questions, the depth of consciousness from which we ask corresponds directly to the depth of answer we receive. When we are facing a challenge, for example, we may ask, "Why me?", which reveals a victim consciousness, a lack of emotional maturity that blames conditions outside of ourselves for our predicament. Such experiences repeat themselves until we learn to ask more skillful, self-revealing questions such as: "What quality must I cultivate to shift this circumstance? What skills am I being called to develop? What would life have me do here? What can I learn from this?"

While our brain is wired to question, the good news is that our inherent intelligence and intuition are wired to answer. Within every question is an answer endeavoring to reveal itself, which is another way of saying the answer is in the question. The questioner, the act of questioning, and the answer are all part of one unified field. Questioning draws answers into its magnetic field, just as the great scientists, explorers, inventors, philosophers, mystics and everyday people have proven. Questions are our steppingstones to a revelation of a larger existence.

"If you want to be a better believer, ask lots of questions," says Dr. Andrew Newberg, Associate Professor of Psychiatry in the School of Medicine at the University of Pennsylvania and author of *How God Changes Your Brain*. What is your unique way of posing a question to yourself? What do you do when you cannot find answers to the questions that go on marinating within you? Answers to questions like: Who am I? Why am I here? Did I exist before I was born? How did life arise? Is there something more real than the material universe? What does it mean to live a purposeful life?

The busyness of our days does not excuse us to brush off such explorations, leaving them to pundits, philosophers and spiritual teachers to provide answers for us. "Why think about such things when we can just buy a book, attend a seminar, or go to Wikipedia?", we sometimes say to ourselves. We all get that life's pace has escalated. But if we are committed to living full-out on this precious journey we will make it a priority to set aside time to go on an inner quest and seek answers to those questions that never go away.

In the laboratory of my own questioning experiments, this has been my recurring insight: Every answer requires a questioner; therefore, the answer is You! What does that mean, "the answer is you?" Just as electricity cannot function without two poles, positive and negative, questions and answers function similarly—the question is one pole, the answer is the other. Because the answers to your questions are woven into the very fabric of your own inner being, there can be no other answer but You!

At the end of each chapter in this book you will find a reflective exercise which, when practiced with an open mind and heart, will reveal areas within your life structures that are flourishing and those in which inner work remains to be done. These exercises are meant to be of support to you in developing skillful means for fully participating in this wondrous journey called Life.

May whatever you take from this book be of service to you in living your highest potential and becoming a beneficial presence on the planet.

# 1

# THE ANSWER
# IS YOU

As you read this page, other individuals are networking at Internet cafes. Some are jogging through a park where homeless persons lay asleep under the sheltering generosity of a tree. Parents are driving their children to school; others remain at home searching through classified ads. While our outer activities vary, the same questions press against the heart: "How can I have a sense of well-being when life as I know it is dissolving right in front of me? How can I find happiness in such an unpredictable world? Where, oh where, can I find some peace of mind? Is there any solid ground on which to stand?"

Despite seeming obstacles and detours, an inner impulse urges you on, as though you are following a reliable map to that place which holds the answers to these courageous and profound questions. A place that ultimately reveals that because the answer is within you, the answer *is* You! Your relationship with yourself is so multi-layered that it requires a wholehearted commitment to cut through to the core of your being, to the transcendental Self that you are. Some call this the Higher Self, made in the image and likeness of godliness.

The image and likeness of Spirit is both within and beyond its creation. This faculty is also an aspect of our birthright. We are both imminent and transcendent beings: imminent in the world of matter as evidenced through our physical senses, emotions, and thoughts, and transcendent as the non-material Self that simply witnesses. We are empowered to transcend our human characteristics, thus reflecting the image and likeness of the Spirit in which we are made. When we consciously make use of this powerful faculty, we become fully franchised co-creators of our individual and collective human destiny.

Whatever actions you perform, whatever thoughts you think, whatever emotions you feel, the You of you is the impersonal, nonattached Witness of them. Any habitual behavior pattern, personality trait or neurosis that you release from your life is possible because it is not an aspect of your true nature. Only what is Real cannot fall away from you because it *is* you. Just as the Spirit remains changeless, so does your Higher Self remain changeless, a constant amidst the vicissitudes of your life experiences. The You of you is a formless, changeless Reality.

We have a body but we are not the body. We have a mind, but we are not the mind. Body and mind are vehicles through which the Self expresses. Each of us is That which is conscious of having a body and mind. As we abide more and more in our true Self we become empowered to make wisdom-guided choices. Choice is a function of awareness. When we choose to evolve our mindsets and heart-sets then self-empowerment, love, abundance, joy, freedom—all that seems just beyond our grasp or that seems to slip between our fingers—are tapped from within and released into our experience. We do not exist to aggressively get; we are here to tenderly *let* that which is within us to harmoniously flow into our outer life.

Will you give your consent to making a deeper commitment to discover That which has been implanted within you, That which awaits the ripe conditions to leap into full expression as you? This is a courageous and vital commitment, because when the proper conditions are met, who you are fully expresses beyond the ego's to-do list and purposes designed for its glorification. When you wake up it no longer matters who your parents are, how many who's who volumes you appear in, if you've been born into abject poverty or if you are physically challenged. All of that pales into comparison to the emergence of the Perfect Idea that is latent within you.

To make this more visceral, let's say that right now you have in your pocket a rosebush seed that you've forgotten about. Then one day while doing your laundry it falls out of your pocket onto the floor. Out of curiosity you plant it in a small container. After it grows roots and sprouts, you transplant it into your garden. With the proper conditions of sunlight, water, and plant food, what started out as a tiny seed, then a sprout, matures into a rosebush with exquisite blossoms. Obviously, within that seed the perfect pattern of a rosebush existed all along.

Within all beings there is also a seed of enlightenment, a perfect pattern of self-realization awaiting the proper conditions to emerge. Ralph Waldo Emerson, when describing the nature of the human being, was fond of using the word endogenous. "Man is that noble endogenous plant," he would say, "which grows, like the palm, from within outward." Endogenous means "originating internally." (It is the opposite of exogenous, which means "originating externally.") As human beings, we cultivate our consciousness from within and project it outwardly into the world of effects.

Everything about us—how we pick up a pen, how we drive, how we eat, how we maintain our environment, our posture, clothing, voice—is an outer reflection, an advertisement of our inner state of consciousness. This means that as an endogenous being you forge your own identity and destiny. Time comes to you in the form of experiences, as opportunities to make new choices and thus burn old seeds of karmic tendencies in the bonfire of self-actualization. It's up to you, and only you, because you are the answer to the question of when you will wake up to your true nature.

Earlier in this chapter I referred to evolving our mindsets and heart-sets. Mindsets are comprised of our beliefs;

heart-sets are our feelings. When our mindsets and heart-sets become aligned, our desires begin to manifest.

Our mindsets and heart-sets inform our motives, the impetus for our actions. One method for evolving mindsets and heart-sets is to ask empowering questions. Disempowering questions such as "Why me? Why now? Who can I blame for this?", obstruct our evolutionary progress. In contrast, empowering questions take us directly into the heart of our situation: "What quality is asking to be activated within me? What must I release from my mental or emotional patterns to shift this situation?" Such questions press the reset button within our mindsets and heart-sets, creating an opportunity for us to activate our more expansive, compassionate, joyous and wise aspects of being.

Every problem is a question trying to be asked. Every question is an answer seeking to be revealed. Every answer is an action seeking to be expressed. Every action is a way of life endeavoring to be integrated into your experience. Your inner Self yearns to respond to empowering questions such as: "Who am I, and why am I here? What gifts have I shown up on the planet to cultivate and deliver? What must I do to take the next step in my evolutionary growth?"

You are being asked to do away with place-holders of negativity at the table of your consciousness and to replace them with place-holders of confidence in your fundamental goodness, your talents, skills, gifts, and your challenges, which are all invitations to bring forth healing and wholeness. What this means is having the willingness to let go of the knots you've tied yourself into through worry, doubt, fear—mindsets which have no evolutionary or transformational value. For example, some of you will begin reading this book accompanied by worries. As you become absorbed in the subject matter, your worries recede into the background of your awareness. However, when you put down these pages and walk into another room of the house, your mind will go on a hunt for your earlier worrisome thoughts. "Now where was I with trying to figure out how I'm going to…." You will mentally search for the negative place-holder that is storing your concerns. The point is that our worries and problems cannot be solved unless we evolve beyond worry, because our problems cannot be solved at the level at which they occur.

Sometimes when we worry about a situation it is a substitute for taking responsible action. We fool ourselves into thinking that if we are worrying it means we are analyzing the situation until we get a sense of direction. Worry is not an empowering response. Worry is a rehearsal we conduct to prepare our reaction to what we fear might happen. "Oh my God, please don't let this happen," we desperately cry, "but just in case....." Toxic chemicals spill into our nervous system blocking our receptivity to the inner guidance and insights that would lead us out of what we're stuck in.

In contrast, an affirmative place-holder is a tap on your shoulder that says, "Hey, now's the time to pull up that insight you had last week about how life is on your side supporting you, carrying you, cheering you on. Remember, life is trustworthy because Spirit is trustworthy." An affirmative mindset expands our ability to see creative responses to our challenges and enables us to choose actions that result in the highest outcome for all concerned.

Another empowering place-holder is gratitude. Try this and see how differently your day begins: When you wake up in the morning think of three things for which you are grateful. Saturate your awareness with appreciation. Then, let go of the reasons for your gratitude and remain in the affirmative energy that you generated. Let this energy confidently carry you throughout your day. As you make this a daily practice, you will see that your mind finds more and more to be grateful for, which draws even more good into your magnetic field. Appreciation attracts more to appreciate.

I want to make an important point here: The practices described in this book are not methods for creating a way to bypass the challenges we all face in life, to put a happy face on the sorrow in our hearts. Their intention is to provide the skillful means for courageously, compassionately drawing out the best of ourselves when we face challenging times. Instead of resisting them with wishful thinking—"I wish this weren't happening; I wish I were anywhere but where I am and anyone other than who I am"—you will welcome them as a lens through which to see the unconscious thought and behavior patterns that self-sabotage progress, joy, creativity and freedom. So often when we look back on our challenges we realize that they were exactly what we needed to become who we are today. What matters is whether we learn from them or not, whether we choose to continue repeating them or not, whether we use them to enhance our mindsets and heart-sets as we keep moving forward in our evolutionary progress.

Our seeming problems are emblematic of a set of beliefs, perceptions and points of view that no longer serve us. The problems themselves are *not* the problem; they reflect mindsets that stand between us and our natural state of happiness. And speaking of happiness, according to *Psychology Today*, in 2008 4,000 books were published on happiness, up from 50 in 2000. Let us not simply study happiness; let us *live* it!

We are totally equipped to hold a challenge in one hand and hold the means for working with it in the other hand. This was recently driven home to me when my wife Rickie and I were in New York at the United Nations building where I was making a presentation. We had to leave immediately after I closed my talk so that we could catch a plane to our next destination. Just as we were getting into the shuttle to the airport I realized that I'd left my mobile phone inside the assembly hall. I said to Rickie, "I've got to dash back in and….."

"No!" she interjected, "we might miss our plane."

"I have to have my phone," I contested. "It has all my information…I need it…"

"Okay," she relented, "I'll stay in the shuttle while you do your thing."

I practically flew through the first security check and ran down the hallway. Upon spotting a second security guard, I slowed down and walked calmly to the door of the assembly room where I'd just been speaking. To my surprise, there was already a speaker standing at the podium addressing the crowded room. I walked in as though I belonged there and made my way towards the podium. As I approached the front of the room, I nodded at another security officer who, fortunately, reciprocated. "Maybe he remembered me," I inwardly said to encourage myself.

Energized by the fact that my phone was now within a 15 foot grasp, I nodded to security once again. Suddenly, the speaker said something that caused her audience to begin clapping. Taking advantage of that perfect interlude,

I leapt up the few stairs to the small table just behind the podium, rescued my phone and descended just as the clapping had stopped. Once out of the room, I headed rapidly down the hallway, strolled coolly by security, exited the front door and jumped into the shuttle. "On to JFK airport," I directed, as though nothing short of a miracle had just occurred.

About a mile from JFK, I happened to glance at my itinerary. "We're supposed to be at *LaGuardia*! We have to turn around!", I exclaimed.

"What?" the driver asked incredulously, "You said JFK!"

"Yeah, I know, but we've got to turn around. Maybe we can still make our flight." He spun the car around and headed for LaGuardia at what felt far too under the speed limit. "You're going too slow!" Obviously, I was referencing what was occurring in the present.

"You said JFK!", our driver reiterated, still stuck in the past.

Rickie and I chimed in together, "We've got to get to LaGuardia!", which referenced the future.

We continued flashbacking to the past, being in the present, and entering the future, punctuated by Rickie and I breathing deeply and inwardly declaring, "All is well in the nowness of this moment." After what felt like an eternity we arrived at LaGuardia, relieved that we had sufficient time to make our flight. Just as we were about to get out of the vehicle Rickie said, "Give me a kiss." Doubting I'd heard right I asked, "Give you a *what*?" She repeated, " Give me a kiss, right now!"

It's impossible to kiss in the past or future; you can kiss only in the present, which leads to the now. So after the kiss we exited the shuttle in the now-ness of the moment. At last everything had fallen into place. That is, until we got to the check-in counter and were told, "You're at the wrong terminal."

"What?! Our tickets say United Air," I said, to which the clerk responded, "Yes, but operated by *US Airlines*, which is located at another terminal. By the way, you'll need to take a cab there."

We immediately caught a cab, curbed at the proper check-in, got to the gate, only to be advised that the flight was delayed for an hour. So we walked around and shook hands with people while apologizing for being the apparent cause of suspending time and delaying the flight.

During our flight I began contemplating the details of what had just unfolded. Sometimes we think our good or our needs are being delayed. We succumb to impossibility thinking as in, "It's never going to happen. I guess it just can't be done. Maybe it wasn't meant to be." Reset your mindset! When someone sings you an opera in the key of "That's never been done before; your plan is too big; you're too old; you don't have the right credentials," tune it out. Keep such notions from homesteading in your mindset. Tell yourself, "I'm flowing with the evolutionary impulse of the universe. Right action is taking place with grace and ease."

When you sense that you are in a delay pattern, ask yourself these questions: "What is trying to emerge in my understanding? What am I being asked to become in order to move forward? What gift must I activate within myself?" The universe will give you feedback and you will discover that the answer has been within you all along. Know that a delay is not a denial; it simply means that you are gaining some valuable wisdom that you will need going forward.

As I continued reflecting on our human mindsets, I understood that sometimes we don't stop living in the past due to attachments born of pride, denial, or shame. Then there are those who choose to live in the future because of fear or ambition. Individuals living in the present may carry embarrassment and vanity. It is only in the zone of "now" that there are no issues, no worries, fears or doubts. "Now" is a dimension of timeless time and transcendent qualities of being.

Sometimes we vacillate from the past to the future, back to the past, and on it goes. That's the time to command, "Stop!", center yourself within and enter the reality of the now-moment. In that quiet place you will feel a resounding "Yes" empowering your existence, escorting you into the next now-moment with full trust in the fundamental goodness of life.

Anchor your highest purpose on the ground upon which you now stand. Let love, transformation, and trust in spontaneous goodness be your place-holders. Your heart knows how to trust because it is something you are born with. First and foremost, know who you are as an endogenous being who actualizes the infinite possibilities that lie within you. *You are the very answer you seek.*

## *Aligning Your Matrix*
## *of Mindsets and Heart-sets*

Are you *really* who and what you think you are, or have you cultivated mindsets and heart-sets that derail you from identifying and expressing your authentic Self? The following introspective exercises are designed to lead you into an exploration of your mindsets and heart-sets which will reveal how you currently perceive and experience yourself, and how you may introduce yourself to deeper dimensions of your being. You will need a pen, paper, and a location where you will have quiet and privacy.

1. Who do you think you are? What qualities define the person you perceive yourself to be? Create this list spontaneously, with what immediately comes to you before you can edit or censor it.

2. Review your list of qualities. Do you want to be other than who and what you presently think you are?

3. Considering how the power of your thoughts forms the matrix of your relationship with yourself, what new

mindsets would support the ways in which you wish to grow and develop?

4. How do you feel about yourself? What is your heart-set about who you perceive yourself to be? What would you add or delete in your heart-set that would reveal more truth about who and what you are?

5. What success-seeds would you like to plant in your mindsets and heart-sets to impact your life structures: mentally, spiritually, physically, professionally, financially, socially, creatively? For example, what mindset would you like to develop to support yourself in more fully delivering your gifts in your life structure of livelihood? What heart-set would you have to cultivate to accept that you deserve to fully deliver your gifts?

# 2

# TAPPING THE ROOT OF HAPPINESS

Who among us does not yearn to be happy? Philosophy, religion and psychology reveal humanity's efforts to define the meaning of happiness, how to experience it and how sustain it. While traditions and beliefs individuate one culture from another, the desire for happiness is the common denominator uniting all beings. "I believe that the very purpose of our life is to seek happiness," says His Holiness the Dalai Lama. Aristotle put it this way, "Happiness is the meaning and the purpose of life, the whole aim and end of human existence." When viewed through the lens of "the answer is *you*," we see that happiness has nothing to do with forces outside of ourselves because we are the producers of happiness as it outpictures in our life structures.

We cannot escape a sense of entitlement where happiness is concerned, and for good reason: happiness is embedded in our essential nature. So how do we walk confidently towards being genuinely happy? The discovery of our innate joy is a conscious inquiry, art, and discipline. Now don't let an old relationship with the word "discipline" throw you, because it's a beautiful word. The word *discipline* shares the same root as *disciple*, meaning one who is in the process of being ready to learn. We are all disciples of happiness, so let our practice begin.

Genuine happiness cannot be bought or sold. It cannot be forced upon us nor can we force it upon others. No one can give us happiness or take away our misery. As Paramahansa Yogananda taught, "No one can make you happy if you want to be unhappy, and no one can make you unhappy if you want to be happy." Every individual must give his or her own consent to being happy.

Unhappiness is also a choice, evidenced by individuals who are addicted to constant grumbling and complaining. As a simple example of how little it takes to get us hooked, consider pet peeves. Woe unto that person who triggers our pet peeves! Whether it's someone who gets in front of us in the "10 items or less" grocery checkout line and actually has a minimum of 18 things loaded into his cart, or the individual who dashes into our parking place just as we are getting ready to turn into it, we can make ourselves miserable over our pet peeves. We'll even devote 15 precious minutes complaining about such events to a friend on the phone. As Gurdjieff, a Russian teacher and mystic observed, "A man will renounce pleasure, but he will not give up his suffering." Strangely, negative individuals live in a paradox where unhappiness gives them a sense of false happiness. Have you ever had a person affirm your suffering, yet accuse you of being in denial when you indicated you still felt a sense of well-being in the midst of it? Perhaps it is this mindset that gave birth to the saying "misery loves company."

On an occasion when I was speaking on the subject of happiness a conference participant asked, "Why is it that when I do things that are supposed to make me happier I just feel more empty?" When I asked him what those things included, he described a long list of activities—hobbies, working out, seminars, social outings and things of that nature. What is clear, I shared, is that external events are neutral; they don't in themselves produce happiness. It's the consciousness in which we participate in activities that makes the difference. The more we experience the richness of the inner Self, the more we bring happiness to the outer aspects of our life.

Sometimes what is required is to redefine, to reframe our definition of happiness. Happiness is not the absence of sadness. Sadness is the complement to happiness. It is absolutely possible to remain happy while being aware that sadness is passing through us.

We have somehow bought into the belief that sadness is a synonym for depression. The collective mind of our society has reached a consensus that the slightest onset of sadness requires an immediate remedy, be it a medical prescription or the self-medication of our choice. This is a misunderstanding. Sadness can open our hearts, touch our soft spot and gift us with compassion for our own and the challenges of others. It can open us to our true feelings so that we can begin working with them; it can create space for qualities of mind to manifest such as patience and loving-kindness for ourselves and others. Sadness is a doorway to profound growth and self-awareness. We can simultaneously experience sadness and grieve our losses knowing that we have everything we need within us to see us through, to support us as we use skillful means to navigate the ever-changing terrain of life. In contrast, genuine depression brings impairment in our work, self-care, and social activities, and requires professional attention.

That real happiness is not conditioned by outer circumstances is a fact that cannot be overstated. Dostoevsky's insight reveals how we may actualize this unconditionedness: "In suffering, look for happiness." Any day of the week we can read or hear about everyday people who have been elevated to heroes and heroines because they maintained their joy and zest for life amidst circumstances that were anything but happy. Did they possess skills superior to the average person? No. They tapped into the inexhaustible deep roots of happiness within the human spirit, roots that transcend life's external conditions and cannot be destroyed by the dust and grit of the journey. Nothing and no one can remove the fountain of happiness that is our ground of being. Nor can they interrupt its flow. We hold the key to freedom in our hands when we become aware that we alone are responsible for our state of being.

When we are happy our hearts and minds are open, receptive, flexible, creative and teachable, qualities that are prerequisites for success. As we begin to consciously choose happiness as a way of life we are led to the realization that joy is our natural state of being. Happiness enriches us. Happiness generates more happiness.

Now happiness isn't simply about decorating the ego, such as adding a new credential after our name, collecting award plaques for our walls, fame or fortune. As lovely and rewarding as these experiences are, they give only superficial, temporary pleasure. Happiness is not about acquisition, such as when we buy a new car. For weeks after we drive our prized possession off the lot we enjoy that wonderful aroma of "newness" that hits the olfactory nerves each time we enter our vehicle. Soon enough, however, that pleasant fragrance turns into the smell of stale green tea and we must begin looking for a replacement. So let us not confuse happiness with pleasure. Pleasure is temporary, fleeting, whereas happiness is a constant.

When the energy of our thought-forms radiates out into life, universal law responds. Whether we are conscious of it or not, we are given constant feedback from the Universe. If your thought-form of happiness is owning a TV screen that is bigger than your overall vision for your life and the TV breaks down, then you have lost the source of your happiness. Certainly we are to enjoy the pleasures of human existence, but grasping at material baubles or being constantly entertained so that we can remain anti-bored until we die cannot substitute for the unconditional happiness that comes from consciously participating in a co-creative relationship with the Spirit, and living in alignment with the harmonic laws governing the universe.

So what are the inroads to such a relationship? First, we tap directly into the root of our inherent joy through time-tested practices such as meditation, affirmative prayer, contemplation, spiritual study, Life Visioning and selfless service. In this way we imbue our egoic, mental, physical, financial, professional, communal, relational, and spiritual life structures with that joy. Harmonious relationships, creativity, prosperity and generosity of heart become the hallmarks of our outer successes.

A second way is to move through life with an affirmative point of view, a "yes" approach, which maintains an openness and receptivity to the field of infinite possibilities. A person whose life-view is affirmative radiates a glow from within that is highly magnetic and contagious. Luminosity radiates from an authentically happy individual and cannot be extinguished, hijacked or robbed by external circumstances.

The third way is to realize that we are on the planet to deliver our gifts, talents and skills without attachment to the outcome. When we remain nonattached we go beyond mentally limiting our good to that which we are convinced we need to be happy. The bane of human experience is that human beings think they know how the Universe should answer their prayers. As I teach in the Life Visioning Process and in my book *Spiritual Liberation*, we are here not to *make* something happen; we are here to *let* ourselves be available as a distribution center for that which is possible on a cosmic level. This can be a challenge to goal setting, which always seeks a successful outcome that makes us look and feel good. Our part, however, is to make our delivery with all the passion, creativity, intelligence and nonattachment that we can, to offer it as an unconditional gift that seeks no reward, that has no agenda other than to give of itself.

The fourth way to genuine happiness is to drop our false sense of self-importance, our egoic notions that the world revolves around us. Just as it was believed that the sun revolved around the Earth until modern science proved the Earth revolves around the sun, so is the fallacy that happiness revolves around an egocentric way of life giving way to a new paradigm that happiness is a worldcentric way of life. When we slow down our speedy mind we become more present and mindful of how we can reach out to support others right on the spot, which can be as simple as taking the time to open a door for someone to saving a life. Arrogance is replaced by humility; self-absorption is replaced by the realization of our interconnectedness to our world family. Being of service to others is welcomed as an opportunity to open and expand the heart beyond the narrow confines of living life on the "me plan."

According to a Harvard University study that looked at nearly 5,000 individuals over a period of 20 years, happiness spreads through social networks like an emotional contagion. When an individual becomes happy, the report claims, the effect can be measured to have spread up to three degrees and to last for up to one year. "We've found that your emotional state may depend on the emotional experiences of people you don't even know, who are two to three degrees removed from you," says professor Nicholas Christakis of Harvard Medical School, who co-authored the study with James Fowler from the University of California, San Diego.

Gratitude is the fifth way to tap into the wellspring of happiness. It is interesting to observe how often our attention goes to what we don't have, while gratitude for what we do have is pushed into the background. Gratitude heals the spiritual astigmatism of lack and limitation; it clarifies the mind so that we may see the opportunities and possibilities which abundantly surround us. The saying that "opportunity only knocks once" is the product of a limited understanding of the generosity of the Universe. Gratitude is acceptance of the Good that is ours when we know ourselves to be worthy of receiving it.

The natural urge of the human being is to share. Generosity takes us directly into the heart of happiness because it gives expression to our oneness with every man, woman, and child gracing the planet. When we hear on the news or read about individuals who, on a global scale, share their wealth to uplift the lives of others, it is very moving and inspiring. Equally or even more touching is how everyday people in our local community send donations or items to support a perfect stranger whose plight they just learned about on the news, a person from whom they will receive no public acknowledgment of their givingness. We may think to ourselves, "I'd like to do such a wonderful thing." The truth is that each of us *can*. Whether it's a dollar given with a loving heart or millions of dollars to an organization that feeds a nation, the universe rejoices.

Harvard researchers conducted another study that showed how giving—no matter how simple in form— is such a potent immune booster that it can be experienced just by watching someone else in the act of giving. What a powerful statement about our interconnectivity! In this well-known experiment, students watched a film of Mother Teresa as she tended the sick in Calcutta. When tested, even those who insisted they weren't particularly fans of Mother Teresa had increased their immune function.

A person filled with happiness is one who has captured a vision for his or her life that is beyond living on the "me and mine" plan. When our purpose in life encompasses more than fulfilling our individual desires and includes the happiness of others, we will know the meaning of true wealth. Through heartfelt acts of generosity we create and sustain a cycle of happiness, and the happiness we give to others returns to us multiplied abundantly.

Considering all the challenges we are currently facing in our world, happiness may seem a frivolous intention. We cannot deny the circumstances and events human beings are grappling with at this time in our history. Any meaningful discussion about happiness cannot ignore the pains of war, genocide, slavery, human trafficking, immigration challenges, AIDS, economic collapse, starvation, poverty, or the depletion of Earth's resources. And yet when we examine the lives of individuals who have made and continue to make a tremendous impact in forwarding the causes of justice, peace, and honoring the dignity of all beings—luminaries such as Nelson Mandela, Dr. A. T. Ariyaratne, Mother Teresa, Gandhi, Thich Nhat Hanh, Martin Luther King, Jr., the Dalai Lama—we see that in spite of their endless challenges they maintained their inner equanimity, their integral happiness. Remaining attuned to their inner core of happiness gave them the perseverance, the compassion, the courage and strength to forge ahead despite seemingly impossible obstacles. They demonstrate for us how inner joy can be experienced in the midst of extraordinarily challenging situations, and that what they have done so may we do, each in our own simple yet impactful way.

Let us all take heart knowing that right on the ground where we now stand we may anchor happiness on the planet and share it with all with whom we come in contact.

## *At Play in the Field of Happiness*

The following exercises are designed to begin an inner inquiry into your relationship with happiness and amplifying its presence in your life structures.

Begin by finding a quiet place where you won't be interrupted for at least twenty minutes. You will need a pen and paper, or may use a computer if it is located where you will have quiet and privacy. Next, take the following questions in the order presented and write down the first thing that comes to your mind without censoring or editing your responses. You may want to center your awareness by taking a few long breaths before you begin.

1. What is your definition of happiness? What are the sources of your definition? Does your current definition conform or conflict with what you have been conditioned to believe about happiness?

2. What behaviors result form your definition of happiness? Do they create peace, harmony, generosity of heart? What is required to align your definition of happiness with your actions?

3. How do you handle challenges that arise? Are you happy with the results?

4. Name three actions you may take right now to increase your happiness quotient. What qualities would you have to cultivate to support these actions? What mental habit patterns would you have to release to support them?

# 3

# HARMONIZING YOUR LIFE STRUCTURES

Inherent within our mind, heart, and spirit reside powers and capacities that became ours the moment we were conceived in the mind of Spirit. Knowing what they are is not sufficient; we have to *consciously activate and apply* them. As we do so we weave a tapestry of harmony into our life structures. Upon hearing me say this in a class I was teaching at the Agape University of Transformational Studies and Leadership, a student enthusiastically interjected, "I like being in control of my life because it makes me feel strong, like I'm on top of my game, so how can I start using the kind of power you're talking about?" Although this student was eager to begin, his motive—control—is incapable of bestowing authentic empowerment.

I can remember almost getting snagged by a similar approach, but as I matured I realized that control is repression or suppression masquerading as self-discipline, or that a person "has it all together." Control also can be used to armor ourselves against pain and to avoid the vulnerability of letting in the love, kindness, compassion, and generosity expressed towards us. *Control is an illusion rooted in the ego. Surrender is alignment with the inner spirit.* The great Sufi mystic Rumi put it this way: "Cut off those chains that hold you prisoner to the world of attachment." Ego likes the status quo, a business as usual approach which imprisons us through attachment to our familiar habit patterns, our way of perceiving and doing things. When our inner spirit has sway over our perceptions it expands our view, our choices, and illuminates our actions.

Self-surrender shows up as confidence in our fundamental goodness, our core essence of being, which makes us open and receptive to inner guidance from our natural wisdom. When we are confused about the source of genuine empowerment, we think and act in ways that create more confusion and chaos in our life structures. Each of us can set an intention to cultivate skillful means, motivated by the possibilities of what awaits us when we do.

Life structures are the outer aspects of our life in which our inner growth and development, or lack of it, show up. The stability of our life structures corresponds directly to our state of our consciousness. We stabilize and harmonize our life structures through a conscious desire to do so, which leads us to practices that support our intention including meditation, affirmative prayer, introspection, spiritual study, Life Visioning, and selfless service. Harmonization of our life structures frees our time and energy to explore deeper dimensions of our being.

Our fundamental life structures include ego, mental, spiritual, livelihood, relationship, physical (body temple), financial, and communal aspects of our existence. We naturally want meaning in our life beyond handling the requirements for survival, so let us begin with a description of the most basic life structure—ego—which will be followed with the rest in no hierarchical order.

**Ego:** When the ego structure is in a state of well-being it expresses as healthy self-care, self-trust, self-respect, self-love, self-expression. When our ego is unhealthy we experience an existential crisis of meaning and look to the outside world for validation. Someone gives us a compliment and our heart soars; our mind recites it throughout the day. Praise and blame determine our happiness factor. We are victims of the world of appearances and constantly compare ourselves to others. Am I being appreciated enough? Will the next self-help book I read finally make me happy? Will those new boots make me look cool? Did that person just look enviously at my new car? We live life swimming on the superficial waves of egoic self-importance, diving into fearful depths of questioning our worth and value in the world. Our imagination feeds on the fantasy of the happiness we will experience once the outer world has convinced us of our greatness. Only when we are recipients of the world's applause—at least from those in *our* world— can we finally deserve to relax into self-acceptance.

When our ego is healthy there is no experience of either inferiority or superiority. We don't live comparing ourselves to others, envying who they are or what they possess. We realize our intrinsic precious worth. We know we are cherished by Existence, by our Source, and our self-love is a reflection of that realization. A healthy ego is self-aware and self-disciplined. Then, when the trickster aspect of ego attempts to seduce us, we recognize its approach and don't act on its suggestions.

A healthy ego makes a decision to spend less time in negativity and more time in listening to the Higher Self. When we loosen the ego's grip and listen instead to our innate wisdom we move forward with clear seeing and wise action. An unhealthy sense of "me and mine" will metamorphous into "thou and thine." A healthy ego is one that has transcended the incessant desire to separate into "we and them," so that what prevails is no longer a sense of separation but rather a sense of oneness with the Whole.

Another aspect of mental and emotional health as expressed through the ego's sense of "I-ness" is that we are comfortable being alone, we are at home in our own presence without grasping for entertainment to avoid ourselves. We are able to use this alone time for introspection, reflection, contemplation, and spiritual study.

**Livelihood:** This life structure is beyond having a job. Livelihood is the expression of our creative purpose, a vehicle for our gifts, talents and skills to make a contribution to the planet. When we work consciously with this life structure we see the ways in which we hold back expressing our creativity and begin to develop the courage to fully share our gifts. We may find it necessary to change our profession as we uncover areas in which we have been hiding out. This very capacity that we have for self-observation gives us the power to make new choices. Instead of allowing mental laziness or self-depreciation to prevent us from identifying our right livelihood, we become enthusiastic about sharing our talents, gifts and skills in fulfillment of our highest potential.

There are specific mind-traps we can fall into here. For example, we may have a natural talent for painting. Because of this, we assume our right livelihood is that of an artist. So we become adherents of the "do what you feel passionate about and the cash will follow" mentality. Meanwhile, we aren't making enough money to cover our living expenses as we wait for the "cash will follow" part to kick in. Or perhaps we received a college degree in a profession that at this stage in our life no longer serves our higher purpose.

There are many aspects of livelihood to contemplate. No doubt each of us has a concept of what it means to be passionately engaged in our livelihood. What do you mean when you say, "I want to live my passion"? Is passion the same as purpose? Does passion sometimes derail you from your purpose or other responsibilities?

When we invite the song in our soul to freely flow through us we are no longer "working"; we are co-creative partners with Source. If we are a singer we cry out, "I don't just want to sing a song. I offer my gift as a source of inspiration and upliftment." Artists and poets will rise up and say, "My aspiration is for my paintings, my sculptures, my books, my poetry to be a vehicle of awakening." Physicians and healers will exclaim, "Let my skills reveal healing and wholeness." Farmers and individuals in the trades will say, "Use my hands and creativity to create health and nutrition, order and beauty in the world." Business people will say, "Let my products and services contribute to the betterment of the planet."

**Relationship:** Life is in a love relationship with itself. It is this undercurrent of Divine Love that sustains all spheres of existence and stimulates our individual desire to give and receive love, the centerpiece of all relationships. This life structure is about cultivating our ability to offer unconditional love, beginning with our relationship with ourselves, extending it to our loved ones, then expanding it to include all humanity. Relationship is an acknowledgment of our interconnectedness with all beings.

Relationship's blessing is how it functions as a mirror reflecting back to us our more evolved qualities as well as our neuroses. Relationships are places where we grow together in ways of mutual support. As each individual seeks to become more of his/her authentic self, a deep appreciation and respect arises for all that is shared and exchanged within the relationship. When our relationship life structure is healthy we no longer seek relationships to make us happy; instead, we bring happiness to our relationships. In relationship we find the means to stretch into a level of maturity where we cease to consider and protect our own territory first. We are no longer a one-way street where all the directional arrows point towards "me." Instead of asking, "Where can I find someone to love me?", we ask, "How can I radiate more love into my relationships?"

Today we hear a lot about "sacred" love relationships. What exactly makes the love that exists between two people sacred? Certainly sacredness does not occur simply by being in a relationship. Our ability to participate in a sacred relationship has largely to do with how we relate to Existence itself. If life is viewed as sacred, then our relationships will be entered into with the awe, respect, and sense of privilege that conveys an energy of sacredness. Sacred relationship is an encounter with the Spirit with skin. When a groundswell of love overwhelms our entire being, how natural it is to want to hold the entire world in love's embrace.

Relationship takes us off living on the "me plan." It is a dance of purification and expansion. The vibration of intimate love two individuals express towards one another extends beyond the confines of selfishness—it becomes a blessing to the planet.

We are here to learn how to swim together in an ocean of love, peace, joy, selflessness, integrity, cooperation, collaboration, in short—oneness. With this mature perspective our relationships cease being places where we seek to make a deal or manipulate another person into giving us what we think we require to have our needs met. Instead, our relationships become places where we grow together through mutual support. Each individual is supported in finding ways of becoming more of their true self. In healthy relationships individuals *relate*. In the mirror of relating we get a more accurate look at ourselves and are offered an opportunity to do profound inner work.

A beautiful description of genuine love appears in Stephen and Ondrea Levine's book, *Embracing the Beloved*. A conscious relationship "…allows a mystical union of such intensity that relationship is no longer differentiated between I and other, but united with all that is. It enters the mystery of pure awareness and pure love as being indistinguishable. It goes for broke." Going for broke requires courage and releasing our octopus grip on our fearful, hungry little ego and surrendering our vulnerability to love's alchemy.

And one more thing. I can't speak to relationship without mentioning the role of forgiveness. Relationship functions as a laboratory where our neuroses come into microscopic view. Forgiveness arises from compassion for what we see and softens our hearts towards others and ourselves. It allows us to make space for our sometimes clumsy efforts, our missteps, as we practice learning how to love unconditionally.

**Physical (Body Temple):** This life structure concerns our degree of reverence for the physical body as a vehicle of our Spirit. Our level of bodily self-care reveals our relationship to our body. Good health and bodily strength allow us to live our life's vision without the body being an obstacle. It is important, however, to underscore that there are individuals who, in spite of tremendous physical challenges, accomplish great things in their personal life and in their contributions to the world. We hear about such persons—young and older alike—on the news, read about them in books, and perhaps find them living right next door to us or within our own household. Through a clear realization of their purpose, nothing stands in the way of what they have come to fulfill in this lifetime. Such persons are a great inspiration.

There are many views on how to create and maintain physical health, what constitutes a healthy diet, the ideal amount of exercise—you get the idea. My own relationship to health and vitality begins with an inner attitude of gratitude. All it takes is a little study of anatomy, biology and physiology to appreciate the miracle that is our physical body. From there it's not a huge leap to want to care for it so that it may operate at its optimum level.

So the first vital habit is to provide ourselves adequate hydration from clean, pure water. The second is good nutrition, which has to do with eating live foods that carry life force and the light of the natural world. The third is exercise, which benefits us with proper circulation, assimilation, elimination and stimulates the secretion of mood enhancing endorphins. The fourth is detoxification, which includes drinking only liquids or eating less than we normally do at least one day of the week in order to give the digestive system a rest. (Of course speak to your healthcare provider or a nutritionist to learn what kind of cleansing program would work best for your body type and health history.) The fifth is rest, down time. The body needs a time out to replenish and repair, which is accomplished during rest and relaxation. Although we are equipped with the capacity to consciously generate energy, let us be mindful that rest is power.

From a spiritual or metaphysical point of view, the practice of forgiveness once again becomes our ally. Forgiveness purifies our heart and mind which in turn affects the body. I recommend making forgiveness the sixth ingredient that adds to your physical well-being.

I offer my definition of forgiveness here: Forgiveness is the conscious letting go of animosity, resentment, hate, blame, rancor or indifference to another being or oneself. When left unaddressed, the intangible energy of such emotions affects our perceptions, speech, behavior and experiences. This is true even when un-forgiveness seems justified. An accumulation of un-forgiveness becomes toxic in the body.

Sometimes we hesitate to forgive because we presume that it lets individuals off the hook of accountability. At such times we forget that there is a cosmic law of justice that may grind more slowly than we feel is appropriate; however, it does grind surely, as in what we send out returns to us. Therefore, it is a path of higher wisdom to take responsibility for cleaning our inner household of the toxin of un-forgiveness. Forgiveness is often what the heart is waiting for in order to release the past and move into the now-moment.

Once forgiveness becomes an active component of our spiritual, emotional, and physical health regime, we may practice the seventh step, which is accepting the reality that we live in a friendly, trustworthy, and supportive universe. When we wake up every day sensing and knowing that Existence itself is cheering us on, we naturally accept life's possibilities, and infinite are the possibilities.

**Financial:** This life structure is about the realization that we are sourced by Cosmic Abundance. Basically, a consciousness of abundance is one that relates to prosperity as a state of awareness that knows, and knows that it knows, that all needs are met. This energetic carries a trusting vibration of limitlessness, rather than a vibration of lack and limitation which fosters acquisition and hoarding. As beings who have come forth from oceanic vastness, we swim in a sea of Cosmic Good.

This structure is about the realization of our true Source and our sense of worthiness in accepting that we are supported by a loving, generous Universe. Money is an energy exchange that supports us in living our vision and contributing to the good of others. Stabilizing this structure makes us conscious stewards of our financial resources as we participate in the law of circulation by investing wisely, saving, and conscious giving. *We don't "spend" money because with such an approach money runs out. Instead, we circulate money and understand that what we circulate returns to us multiplied abundantly.* The laws of circulation and prosperity are thoroughly explored in Chapter 4, "Embodying True Abundance."

**Community:** This life structure acknowledges our interconnectedness with all life. When stabilized, the narrow confines of the little self expand to include the world. A full participation in community includes the spiritual, social, and political aspects of life and embraces the entire planet as our community. We know ourselves to be world citizens and include the good of all beings in our own. This life structure and our participation in it is examined in detail in Chapter 5, "Becoming an Emissary of Peace."

You may wish to create life structure categories that aren't included here. My intention in this chapter is to address those that most influence our day-to-day existence and interactions with ourselves and others, to enlarge our awareness of both their obvious and subtle aspects, and illustrate ways in which we may live our highest potential as spiritual beings having a human incarnation.

## *Harmonizing Your Life Structures*

The following exercises are designed as foundations for becoming acquainted with yourself, a prerequisite to harmonizing your life structures. As you prepare, gently begin to enter the sanctuary of self and appreciate all that you discover there, no matter what.

**Ego:** With introspection we can relax our grip on the ego that struggles so mightly to protect its sense of being a separate self. Like a holistic physician, we may examine ego and discover what medicine leads it to good health.

1. Under what circumstances does your ego become most triggered and react defensively? What events in your earlier conditioning instilled those triggers? Can you imagine yourself detaching from this history, dropping the story line and responding from an authentically empowered place within you?

2. What is your self-talk following an egoic eruption? Are you able to take responsibility and make amends, first

with yourself, with another when appropriate? Are you able to forgive yourself and others?

3. Considering the ego's purpose is to protect, in what ways may you skillfully direct its energy?

**Livelihood:** Livelihood is more than making money to support ourselves; it is an expression of our innate creative energy. Every act is creative, so whether we are stocking shelves or running a Fortune 500 company is not the issue. It is the consciousness in which we perform our work that determines its artfulness, its integrity.

1. What is your definition of success? What choices and behaviors result from your definition? Do they create inner peace and contentment? What are the sources of your definition? Do you still agree with them?

2. Is your current profession satisfying to you? Would you like to change your source of livelihood? If so, what would it be? What quality would you have to cultivate to bring this change about? What would you have to release to bring it about?

**Relationship:** This life structure is loaded with the potential for experiences that vacillate between tremendous fulfillment and disappointment, depending upon our emotional, mental, and spiritual maturity. Much of our conditioning has us searching for someone to love us or meet our needs. In truth, relationship is about participating in a field of loving awareness that is larger than the individuals involved.

1. Let yourself contemplate whom you show up as in your relationships. Notice your most prevailing attitudes. Are you controlling, manipulative? Are you clingy, needy, or operating from a fear of abandonment or loss? Or are you loving, generous, open to growth? A combination thereof? Just notice without judgment how you relate in the relationships that are currently in your life.

2. How would you feel if you realized that you could never lose love? Describe who and how you would experience yourself in relationships from that love-energetic.

3. Are you asking, "Who will love me?", or "How can I radiate love?"

**Physical (Body Temple):** The body temple is the vehicle of our Higher Self and is precious. How we relate to and care for the body temple is an indicator of our self-care and self-worth.

1. How do you relate to you body? Do you value outer appearance more than inner health? Are there any physical addictions or behaviors that require your loving attention?

2. If there are any changes you wish to make in this life structure, what quality would you need to develop? What habits would you need to release?

**Financial:** To the degree that we are not caught up in financial worries we are able to direct our energies towards living our life's purpose, cultivating the wealth of our inner spirit, and creating prosperity in our outer life.

1. What would your life look like if you possessed everything you believe you require to consider yourself abundant? Describe it without letting your ego censor you.

2. Is your definition of abundance primarily material, or does it include the inner riches of joy, love, peace—intangible qualities?

3. What belief systems have contributed to your relationship with money? Do you circulate money from a place of lack, or from a sense of trust that your needs are met?

4. If you feel a sense of lack, what quality is asking to emerge in your consciousness? What would you need to release to enter an awareness of your innate abundance?

**Community:** Community is an extension of ourselves and a place where we can grow our hearts and spirits, where we can live and interact beyond the narrow confines of the little self. Community offers us opportunities to stretch and cultivate a spirit of humility and generosity.

1. How do you relate to and serve the larger community? Ask yourself: Where am I to deliver my

gifts, talents, skills, to make my contribution to the larger world?

2. What inner practices must I apply to expand my heart and grow my spirit of generosity?

# 4

# EMBODYING TRUE ABUNDANCE

---

Abundance. Is it new age fluff, or a genuine science? Do you need to work hard for it, or is it as simple as ordering the "special of the day"? Do you question why you do or don't have what society considers the accouterments of the good life? Or do you wag your finger in a tsk-tsk gesture because you believe money is the root of all evil? Is wealth about the power of thought, luck, fickle fate? Karma—good or bad?

The plethora of books written on various abundance themes—from how you can have it all, how to get rich quick, the law of attraction, to foolproof investment strategies—have a seductive effect on the human psyche. And for good reason: *There is a cosmic principle supporting our enthusiastic foray into the terrain of abundance.* For simplicity's sake, I call it the "What and Who" principle.

Let's begin with the "What," which I define as an Ineffable Presence that is omnipresent and omni-active, meaning that there is no place where it is not and no activity that is not animated by its Life Force, the cosmic motor running the universe.

The invisible What condensed itself into visible form and is conscious of itself within every atom of creation. We don't fly off the planet because the What has provided the law of gravity. Nothing stands still; all creation is in a constant state of flux because of the evolutionary impulse governing the universe. Cosmic laws are keepers of universal order. This "What" is called by many names: Life Force, God, Brahma, Spirit, Love-Intelligence. Regardless of the names we give to this Great Something as we perceive it and so that we may relate to it, we may be confident that it is always active on our behalf as it seeks to articulate itself in, through, and as us.

We cannot avoid the What. Every time we appreciate the beauty of nature, the love and generosity of another person, the intelligence of science, the inspiration of artistic expressions, the wisdom of our spiritual teachers, we are looking straight into the face of the

What. When we commune with our Higher Self we are in direct contact with the indwelling What. Clearly, it is not about our "becoming" something; it is about discovering, accepting, and expressing what is already true of us. Isn't this a perfect reason to join in the cosmic dance of celebration that is going on in every speck of space?

Next is the "Who," the individualized expression of the What expressing as all sentient beings. As such, we are the beneficiaries of its wisdom, love, beauty, intelligence, compassion, bliss, peace, joy, and abundance that comprise our birthright. We exist as unique emissaries of this beatific vision of the Infinite as us.

Because the What seeks to express its qualities through the Who, we have an inner impulse to seek and manifest its quality of abundance. Whether its ruling a country, coaching a sport's team, living in a prestigious zip code, running a homeless shelter, or renouncing the world in a Himalayan cave in monk's robes possessing only a begging bowl—these are examples of how our inner impulse to acquire abundance expresses according to our state of consciousness.

Individuals who manifest material wealth but lack knowledge of their true nature or how the laws governing the universe operate tend to seek abundance through a consciousness of "the ends justify the means," meaning whatever it takes to increase their bottom line of "more." Those who acquire abundance through honest means but are unaware of their true nature or universal laws tend to be convinced that their accomplishments are merely the result of hard work, good investments—in other words, through outer sources. Then there are persons who rob money or goods to fulfill their desires for abundance because in their state of consciousness they cannot imagine getting it any other way. Others steal not because they want to but to meet basic survival needs within their given circumstances. All of these are ways in which abundance is sought in its more gross form, common form, and survival forms.

A more skillful "how" is demonstrated by those who have done some exploration of metaphysical or mystical principles so have begun to evolve in consciousness. However, if such individuals remain predominantly material-minded, their application of the law of abundance will be used to manifest those things which simply satisfy their ego's desires. They may use the law of attraction but do not understand that it is an entryway into a more profound practice. Not realizing the difference between fulfillment and fill-full-ment, they continue to consume and acquire. But there is never enough of "more." Genuine fulfillment comes from within, from the interior of our being; fill-full-ment comes from without, from the exterior world. Finally, confused and frustrated that outer fill-full-ment has not resulted in inner fulfillment, they eventually begin to search out why, which leads them to the next step in their unfoldment.

The most evolved state of consciousness in which to seek abundance is as a conscious participant in the laws governing the universe, and in such a way that benefits oneself *and* the planet. I like to say that we are not anticipants, we are *participants*. Anticipants live in hope; participants live in trust of the now-moment just as it is. Participants do not wait for the cosmic tumblers to fall into place before they begin living full-out or to win the lottery before they become generous givers.

The laws governing the universe are impersonal and not a respecter of persons. Like electricity, they operate impersonally for all alike. Whether an individual is aware of them or not, or believes in them or not is of no consequence; the laws work independently of our belief in them. However, trust in the laws governing the universe along with conscious participation in applying them is a highly skillful, results-producing combination.

Trust shines the light of awareness on the places in our life where we overtly and subtly hold doubt. Are your doubts based in reality, or are they fabricated mind-constructs? Have you ever observed how your mind carries on a conversation without you? It's as though it gets swept away, gossiping about thoughts, beliefs, opinions, convictions and concepts that have become ingrained into your habituated thought patterns. On they roll, cheered-on by the programming and conditioning of society, parental fantasies, education, and theologies that you've never examined. Finally you realize you were not present, that you had gotten hooked, and your inner observer shouts, "Enough! Come back!"

As harmless as an unexamined life may seem, ignorance is *not* bliss. Ignorance can become a filter through which we avoid things we want to deny, to maintain the status quo, or to avoid the lessons and gifts that life is offering us. Do you ever spin out on thoughts of lack, limitation, doubt, fear, worry, competition, disconnection? Don't let such thoughts go unchallenged. Deconstruct them. Claim your identity as an eternal, infinite being who is no longer subject to the programming of your mind. Affirm that you live, move, and have your being in a field of abundance, that all things are working together for your good. Feel it. Sense it. Know it, because it's true.

In addition to trust, participants also live in gratitude. There are three faces of gratitude. The first is gratitude for all of the good and beauty that is present in our life. The second face of gratitude involves some heavy lifting as we learn to be grateful for our challenges that point out the next stage of our growth. While the surface mind doesn't understand why certain things do or don't come to us, or why they depart from us, participants are grateful that they possess all that is needed to work with situations as they arise. We accept that ultimately all things are working together for our good, that they are invitations to more deeply participate in our ever-evolving consciousness. The third face of gratitude is that we begin to notice that we are in a consistent state of appreciation for seemingly no reason other than the simple joy of existence.

The truth is that we don't have to cultivate a consciousness of abundance; we have only to *discover* what is already ours by birthright. It has not to be sought; it has only to be recognized and accepted. The most direct route to discovering our inner wealth, including abundance, is through meditation. When we commit to consistently practice meditation we commune with the Higher Self, which leads us to the realization that all the qualities required for living a purposeful life, a life that makes us a beneficial presence on the planet, are already ours. Then, as we stand at the center of our existence, we are aware of the Life Force that surrounds us, that interpenetrates all that is, that condenses itself into the form of whatever is needed to meet our needs, into whatever circumstance it is that will lead us to our next stage of growth.

Certainly we cannot deny the poverty we see on the planet. We are in no position to judge those who find themselves in impoverished conditions. In the pop teachings about prosperity there is a shadow side, an immature notion that persons lacking the signs of outer abundance are undeveloped in prosperity consciousness, whereas those who have symbols of abundance possess higher metaphysical knowledge which they use to acquire riches. A deeper understanding will reveal that this is an over simplification. Life is not so black and white. It behooves us to bend our knee in humility before life's mysteries, including why we are born into certain conditions, the changes we undergo in life, and the challenges and blessings that come our way.

What is important to know is that there is a sufficiency of everything required to support those who have less when those who have more understand and participate in the law of circulation. Those who have been born into impoverished conditions where there is insufficient food, clothing, medical care—their needs can be met if the proper conditions emerge in the collective heart of humanity. Whether or not we understand all of poverty's causes, there is a great deal we all can do to assure the dignity of all beings when we compassionately open our hearts, as has been demonstrated by many of the world's humanitarian organizations, philanthropists, and by everyday people.

Now we can't have a straightforward conversation about abundance without including—you guessed it: Money. The "M" word. Generally speaking, when people use words like "prosperity" or "affluence" they are polite substitutes for money. Somehow, in American society it is considered indelicate, impolite, to discuss money in a direct way with anyone other than your broker, banker, accountant and employer! Such is the charge we have around money. Some people fear or abhor money, considering it as the root of all evil. Others are addicted to spending it while others accumulate, hide, and hoard it. As we can see, there are misconceptions and misunderstandings we have about money and its place in our lives. Money is just one face of wealth, and it is supportive to our well-being to have a healthy relationship to it.

Money represents energy. When we give money to someone for a service or product it is an energy exchange. For example, I give you money in exchange for the energy you have invested in landscaping my yard. With that money you pay your daughter's school tuition for which she receives the energy of an education from her teacher. Money is a promissory note in that it is an agreement that energy will be or has been exchanged. Isn't this a far more expansive view than "spending" money? When we spend something it eventually runs out. It becomes spent, as in balance = 0. Conversely, when we circulate energy it keeps cycling back to us as in the truism, "What goes around comes around," which is a simple though accurate description of the law of circulation.

Money itself is neither good nor bad; it is neutral. Money has the meaning we invest in it. For example, in what state of mind do you pay your bills? When bills arrive in your mailbox, how do you receive them? Do you say, "Oh no! How am I going to pay all these bills?" How different it would be if instead you said, "These bills represent an abundance of goods and services that I have already received to enhance my life and I now have the blessing of circulating the energy of money in exchange for them." That was a lot of words, but you get the idea that when you respond in such a feeling tone you shift your relationship to money.

Another habit pattern I've encountered when speaking to people about money is that some individuals want to build a sense of having money from where they're *not*. They say, "Okay, I'm going to use the law of abundance to attract five million dollars because the book I'm reading guarantees that if I can believe it I can achieve it!" That's a bit of a stretch if your bank balance is $125. Sometimes we confuse a hopeful declaration with a powerful affirmation. So we must start where we are and mentally build our "having" muscle.

Regardless of your income level, even if you begin little-by-little, say saving $10 a week, you will provide factual evidence that you "have." When I suggest this sometimes people argue saying, "Well, I don't make much money, so putting a little away each week isn't going to amount to much." If you keep putting $10 away each week, your mind will begin to take ownership of it. "*I have money!*", it will claim, which builds your awareness of having. When we consider the biblical statement that, "To he who has more shall be given, and to he who has not that which he has will be taken away," it is not a religious statement as much as it describes how a consciousness of having relates to the law of circulation. When we radiate a sense of having, more is drawn into that magnetic field. Conversely, when an individual has a sense of lack and limitation, this sets up a magnetic field of loss and not being able to receive the good that is constantly being transmitted by the universe.

Through skillful means we can come into a spiritual, mental, and emotional comfort zone about true abundance. Gratitude for what we have is skillful; generosity is skillful; being a good steward of our financial resources is skillful; expressing our talents, skills and gifts is skillful. These actions are based on wisdom rather than fear, bribery, or a business contract with the laws governing the universe. They are actions based on trust in the givingness of Existence, and trust is a condition of inner relaxation. Dr. Ernest Holmes tells us that, "Prosperity is the outpicturing of Substance in our affairs. We just receive, utilize and extend the gift." This is another way of saying that Undifferentiated Substance takes the form of whatever is needed: health, relationship, livelihood—you get the idea. It is ours to accept, appreciate, and circulate. Let us joyously "extend the gift" by sharing our resources, all the while knowing that we do so from the understanding that there is an inexhaustible supply flowing to us from Source.

When it comes to sharing your financial resources, consider giving to organizations that support the kind of world you want to live in, a world you want your children, grandchildren, all beings to inhabit, and to spiritual teachers and communities that inspire your growth and transformation. Happily, wisely circulate the energy-symbol of money, for in this way your consciousness of abundance matures from metaphysical to mystical, benefiting you and the entire planet.

You live, move, and have your being in a friendly, supportive universe. You are held in an infinite embrace of unconditional love, eternally one with the Whole of existence. As a unique expression of Infinite Possibility, you are here to live an unprecedented life, to live so fully from true abundance that you and those near and dear to you benefit. You are here to be a beneficial presence on the planet, to relish with gratitude all the gifts that the Spirit of life freely offers. Harmonizing your life with a consciousness of true abundance is a very rich place to begin.

# *Exploring and Evolving Your Consciousness of Abundance*

Today and all days remember that abundance is a harmonizing vibration of being and having, not a material vibration of possessing and hoarding. Saturate your awareness with the realization that the universe gives of itself freely, inexhaustibly, and you will neutralize false beliefs in lack and limitation. The following exercises have been designed as a starting point to support you in evolving a consciousness of true abundance.

## *Identifying Your Relationship to Abundance*

1. Define what abundance means to you in your various life structures.

2. Identify any limiting beliefs you have about money, including mental and verbal statements you make to yourself or others about money or finance-related issues. What can you practice from this chapter to shift those beliefs?

3. How does society influence your money beliefs? How have your parents, your life partner, your spiritual beliefs influenced your relationship to abundance and money? What do you need to do to neutralize any negativity and increase positivity?

4. Identify any money challenges you are currently experiencing. What steps have you taken towards working with them? If you have not experienced money challenges, what do you credit it to?

5. If you have children or others whom you influence about abundance and money, what are you communicating to them?

## *Identifying Your Gratitude Factor*

1. Sit quietly with yourself and consider what you are grateful for in life. Write a list of the abundance of things—material and non-material—for which you are grateful.

2. Do you express gratitude to individuals whom you appreciate being in your life? Create a list of their names and by each one list a simple way in which you may extend a gesture of appreciation to them.

## *Identifying Your Generosity Factor*

1. Is there anything that you share anonymously?

2. What do you consciously give to your loved ones, co-workers, spiritual community, the world at large?

3. What would you share if you fully realized that you are a generative being who is fully empowered to manifest true abundance?

4. Do you contribute to your spiritual community, or to the sources of your inspiration and inner growth?

# 5

# LIVING AS AN EMISSARY OF PEACE

On this round planet there are no sides. Boundaries that separate people from people and nation from nation are artificial borders drawn in the sands of time by the human hand. As planetary citizens under the sovereignty of the Great Mystery and the universal laws governing the universe, we have courageously faced many challenges throughout our ever-evolving human history. We humans continue to open our hearts and respond with compassionate action as evidenced by global responses to The World Trade Center tragedy in 2001; the Indian Ocean tsunami of 2004; Hurricane Katrina's devastation in 2005; and the current global ecological and economic challenges of 2009, to name a recent few.

We often stand mute before the awesome mystery of life's unfolding events. There is a place where the mind stops, where philosophical and theological debates and differences have no relevance, where our religious arrogance halts in the face of That which is un-namable, indefinable, unknowable. What is our relationship to this Great Something, and how does it interact with life's horrendous or glorious events? This is what I know for certain: We may rest in the assurance that no experience comes to punish or test us; experiences comes to awaken us. The question is, in life's ordinary and extraordinary occurrences, how are we to align ourselves with the grand design of Existence so that we may become emissaries of peace, vehicles of the evolutionary impulse governing the universe?

Until each of us takes responsibility for our individual biases and prejudices, coming together in heroic gestures of generosity, self-sacrifice or patriotic flag waving will not be powerful enough to permanently shift us into a new paradigm of world peace. Each of us must bravely walk through our own unresolved issues of fear, doubt, worry, insecurity, blame, selfishness, greed, ignorance—all of it! Unless we are willing to do that kind of individual inner work, peace will be only temporary because we will continue to project our own inner shadow onto other individuals and cultures. As the sage Krishnamurti pointed out, "The inward strife projected outwardly becomes the world chaos. After all, war is the spectacular result of our everyday life."

We must free ourselves from the influence of ignorance and prejudices inherent within societal conditioning. What good is nationalism, what good is patriotism if it destroys life itself? If we want to be an individual through whom global-care expresses we must wake up and discover areas where we have become caught or snagged by world opinion, fear, doubt, and aggression, which are contagious responses, and instead express our innate potential for peace, compassion, forgiveness, courage, and love.

Respected harbingers of the world's peace have always been in agreement that stopping the cycle of violence begins with one's relationship with him/herself. If we have a nuclear war going on in our own head we may expect to have a corresponding battleground in the affairs of our personal life. We must get to know ourselves, to open our heart in great honesty. Perhaps we are convinced that our abhorrence of violence prevents us from practicing it. A closer look will reveal that not only do we practice violence on a daily basis, even in subtle ways, we often escalate it in our inner and outer environments. One may be an inner mental terrorist, sending bombs of judgment, anger, animosity or prejudice towards oneself, another person, race, religion or culture in the form of spiteful words, violent actions, or secret thoughts. However and wherever violence expresses it pollutes the environment with the toxic energy of aggression and harm. Aggression is as contagious as any disease, and it can also be healed with the antidote of awakened consciousness, which leads to an enlightened society.

I personally have every confidence in our collective ability to transform our world into one that honors the nobility of all sentient beings, for at no other time in our history has there been such a widespread recognition of the interconnectedness and interdependence of all life. Our undeniable oneness transcends outer religious, cultural, racial, historical, and political differences. Schools of ancient wisdom and contemporary traditions of spirituality alike proclaim our common Source.

We may also thank scientific and technological advancements for the revelation that what occurs in one part of the world causes a ripple effect throughout the globe. For example, during the Viet Nam War in the 60's, our exposure and access to information about events as they unfolded was polarized not only by politics but also the lack of technology. In contrast, the 1991 media coverage of the Persian Gulf War was unique in its instantaneousness. Technology had advanced to the point that this war was broadcast "live" into our living rooms, classrooms, boardrooms, world government headquarters, medical waiting rooms. Today even rural communities are equipped with televisions, computers and cell phones, permitting opinions and responses to form on an independent basis.

The evolutionary impulse of the universe is at work in how cutting-edge science, Face Book, YouTube and Twitter's social-networking are used to share individual aspirations of universal peace. New perspectives on how turbulence may metamorphous into transformation is now part of every day conversation among persons worldwide, thanks to technology. People are getting to know one another not merely through the eyes of their respective society and its government, but on an individual, one-on-one basis, neutralizing opinions conditioned by outside influences.

On occasions when I have been blessed to sit with His Holiness the Dalai Lama, he would ponder if the American people have understood suffering enough to comprehend the deeper meaning of compassion. I understood, of course, that he wasn't in any way wishing suffering on Americans (and his statement was made prior to the tragic events of 9/11). Rather, he was indicating how crisis and its resultant suffering function to provide insights and revelations that become catalysts for change. As I reflected more deeply on his words, I realized that while our country generously provides goods and assistance during international emergencies, in our own backyard we have been able to conduct our business and social lives as usual.

Up until the tragedy of 9/11, much of the American population had experienced a sense of safety which, to some extent, prevented us from compassionately relating to what millions in our world experience as a way of life. Now, eight years later, how can we ever again ignore the suffering of our global brothers and sisters and those in our own back yard? We can no longer afford not to recognize that each of us is an essential part of the collective whole that impacts the entire planet. The questions I ask myself and encourage others to ask are, "Am I willing to do the inner work required to evolve my consciousness into one of unconditional love, compassion, and forgiveness? What work am I to do within myself to heal any sense of separation from the wholeness of life? Am I willing to acknowledge my oneness with all other beings inhabiting the planet?"

I love this statement made by Socrates: "I am not Greek, nor even Athenian. I am a citizen of planet earth." Whether an individual is Irish, Tibetan, Hispanic, Israeli, American, Indian, Palestinian, American or African, the feelings of sorrow, joy, love, loss, grief, compassion— these are felt the same by us all. I have traveled the corners of the world enough to know that playing with the fire of violence creates the ashes of destruction. And yet it cannot be denied that from the ashes of destruction the phoenix of transformation can usher in a society of peacemakers.

We are, even now, capable of employing visionary solutions to challenges such as global warming, war, world hunger, unifying science and spirituality, economic imbalance. The paleontologist and Jesuit priest Pierre Teilhard de Chardin forecasted that the next label for homo sapiens will be "homo progressivus." Buckminister Fuller, a visionary architect and inventor, suggested we would evolve into "hetero-techno sapiens." Whatever the descriptive label, each of us is being called to participate in co-creating the world we wish to see. There is no distinction between one's individual future and the world's future, so the arrow points in the direction of each of us making a choice to live in love rather than fear, to express wisdom over ignorance, peace instead of aggression, and to apply the tools for the evolution of consciousness each of us possesses.

Technology has turned the planet into a neighborhood. Now is the time for our transformation into a sister-and-brotherhood wherein each of us fulfills the mandate to become a beneficial presence on the planet. Individually and collectively our purpose is to expand in consciousness so that Love-Intelligence may download itself through human expression. Emissaries of peace are willing to practice the necessary discipline of the mind and heart to be that expression.

How are we to respond to the universe's mandate to allow peace to find a foothold in our individual hearts so that we may activate the possibilities seeking to express through us? Are we going to remain at the nationalistic level of the meaning of patriotism, the psychological level of exploring the inner causes of violence, or the religious level of what God's will is in world events? Or will our next question be: "If peace begins with me, how can I activate it in my life?" One of our most powerful tools for growth is introspection, examining our beliefs, concepts, perceptions, thoughts, motives, and actions. Exploring the contents of our mind is vital to eradicating mental and emotional habit patterns that undermine healthy, mature thought and action. It is helpful to check in with ourselves, to observe without self-condemnation where an attitude needs adjusting in order to live more compassionately, to make more room in our heart for ourselves and others.

I like to paraphrase this statement of Dr. Howard Thurman: It is impossible to love humanity "in general." Humanity must be loved "in particular," which means that we first learn to love the people right next to us regardless of the color of their skin, the shape of their bodies, their sexual orientation, the religion they practice or their political affiliation.

Just walking down the street looking into the faces of those who pass us by we can instantly observe whether we love "in particular." As we set aside our opinions and look through the lens love, accepting the inherent goodness residing within each individual no matter down dim it seems to be, we accelerate the action of love within them. Then, perhaps instead of winning wars we will begin winning hearts over to peace. When humanity's view transforms egocentric boundaries of "me and mine" into a worldcentric view of "ours," we will have a true chance of creating integrative policies of peace. Harbingers of world peace have taught us that there is no separation between our political endeavors, social endeavors, and spiritual endeavors—all are to be governed by the truth that we are indeed one global family co-creating the destiny of our planet.

Not long ago I was reading *The Three Faces of Power*, a book written by a Quaker, Ken Boulding, wherein he describes the highest form of power as being "integrative power." Integrative power results from choosing actions that open a space for dialogue leading to alignment rather than separation. Isn't it obvious that the global family is at a stage where decision-making must include the good of the whole? Imagine today's world leaders sitting around an executive conference table among self-realized beings such as Buddha, Jesus, Krishna, and Mohammed, all of whom greatly influenced their respective society and culture. It's easy to grasp that these great beings would strongly exhort humanity not to use technological advances, "peace keeping" weapons, and economic sanctions for the peril of humankind. Rather, they would encourage an intelligent expression of oneness, compassion, forgiveness, generosity, and sharing of the world's wealth and resources.

If we are honest, we will admit the tendency of human beings, including ourselves, to respond to life by what enters from the outside. *How we choose to handle our individual responses to life's circumstances also determines the collective international character.* Therefore, we see the same pattern of reacting to what comes from the outside reflected in the world's governments: when a country verbally insults you, insult back; when a country bombs your own, bomb back. It's all from the outside. As we individually and collectively evolve in consciousness we will begin to impact our world from the *inside out* through application of our innate wisdom and love-intelligence. Peace will emerge from the *within* to the *without*. This evolved state of consciousness knows no separation between one's individual good and the good of others, because it is one-and-the-same good! Thus, we move from an egocentric to a worldcentric point of view.

It is clear that returning hate for hate only multiplies hate. Darkness cannot be illuminated by more darkness— it is simply an absence of light, the light of love, compassion, and forgiveness. In our world community we have come to a place where it is inescapable not to love, forgive, or reconcile with our so-called enemies. Hate is injurious to the person who hates, to the nation that promotes hatred. Hate pours toxins into the international bloodstream. We can no longer ignore that hate divides and love unites. Love is the only force capable of transforming. The slogan made popular in the 60's, "Make love, not war," is not some impractical utopian concept. "Of all weapons," said Dr. Howard Thurman, "love is the most deadly and devastating, and few there be who dare trust their fate in its hands."

Many times I have heard the Dalai Lama say that the radicalism of the twenty-first-century is compassion. Forgiving and loving our enemies means we have compassion for the perpetrators of insane violence—not condoning it in any way, but having compassion for persons who would participate in such bloodcurdling acts. There is perhaps no teaching of Jesus the Christ that presents more of a challenge than his instruction to, "Love thine enemies and pray for those who persecute you." Dr. Martin Luther King, Jr. tells us, "The degree to which we are able to forgive determines the degree to which we are able to love our enemies."

The good news is that there is a growing recognition of the wisdom in such statements that violence, war, and prejudice offer no wisdom, no love, no justice, no peace or compassion to our world. Looking back through time we can see that hatred and war have left countries tattered with devastation. When there is violence flowing through the international bloodstream its toxins of ignorance upset the organic balance of the whole. Let us connect the global heart to the global brain and put an end to the ignorance of hatred and violence that cause human suffering.

Dr. John Hagelin, the world renowned quantum physicist who once ran for president of the United States, wrote in his book, *Manual for a Perfect Government*:

> …the experience of pure consciousness corresponds to the direct subjective experience of the unified field of all the laws of nature at the foundation of the physical universe. The influence of positivity and coherence generated by such group practice thus represents an actual physical influence of peace more powerful than any previous defensive technology. If, according to the UNESCO Charter, 'War begins in the minds of men,' then it can easily end in the far more fundamental experience of pure consciousness which underlies and unites us all. The most straightforward, practical implementation of this approach is to establish a 'prevention wing of the military' trained in peace-creating technologies…"

Love is always the winning argument; violence is the language of the inarticulate. "War will cease," Dr. Ernest Holmes tells us, "not when God decides this for us, but when enough people know that it is no longer desirable, and steadfastly maintain their position. From communion with Spirit man will come to perceive the deeper Reality, the broader sharing of the human experience."

As each of us takes responsibility for perceiving the deeper Reality of human oneness and embodying the qualities of an emissary of peace, we will actualize the wisdom of Pythagoras when he said, "Take courage, the human race is divine."

## *Practices of an Emissary of Peace*

Described below are what I call practices of an emissary of peace which include affirmation, prayer, and meditation, along with a forgiveness exercise. I encourage you to apply these tools with loving patience, especially if they are new to you. Awakening, insight, awareness—these cannot be forced. Yet the more we practice, with every step we take on the path of an emissary of peace, we draw closer to self-realization, to seeing with inward sight what has been true about us since the beginning of time. Even if we haven't yet reached the pinnacle of awakening we may lay claim to our inherent state of enlightenment, our candidacy to be an emissary of peace. This calls up our courage, compassion, discipline, joy, and steadfastness so that we do not to give up on ourselves or anyone else.

### *Affirmations of an Emissary of Peace*

**When to practice:** The time to practice an affirmation is whenever you want to or feel you need to. This practice is not limited to challenging times. It is as effective in times of joy and gratitude as it is in times of difficulty.

Affirmations are especially powerful immediately upon awakening in the morning, following a meditation session, and just before falling asleep at night when we are more open and receptive.

**How to practice:** Affirmations can be made silently or verbally. You may prepare your affirmations ahead of time by writing them down or recording them, or you may invite them to arise spontaneously in the language of your heart.

If you wish to sit formally to do affirmations, or following a meditation session, find a quiet area where you won't be disturbed. Sitting on a chair or on the floor, without being rigid, take a position of potency, keeping your back straight and chin parallel to the floor. Next, take a deep inhalation, followed by a long, slow exhalation. Repeat this three times, each time relaxing and letting go into the breath, imagining yourself expanding and connecting to Infinite Life. Keep your awareness conscious and alert so you don't fall asleep.

You may wish to repeat your affirmation aloud a few times to hear, feel, and fully connect with your conviction in the words you either mentally or verbally speak. Next, repeat your affirmation more softly, until it gradually becomes only a mental affirmation. Mentally repeat it until there is a sense of peace, which is the first sign that you are embodying your affirmation.

In case you have never practiced affirmations, the following may assist you with the affirmative energy you want to radiate out from your center of Self. You may select one sentence only, repeating it until you have integrated its spirit. Certainly you may tailor the words to your personal circumstances.

*My consciousness is at peace, for it is now rooted and grounded in the Self. My thinking is spacious, my heart is open and I am established in love, compassion and forgiveness.*

*From the center of my heart, I radiate compassion to all beings knowing they are bathed in the Infinite Love of the Spirit.*

*I awaken the spirit of forgiveness within me. Even now it fills my consciousness with loving kindness towards myself and all beings. I love with the unconditional love of Spirit.*

*Right here, right now, divine love loves through me. Enlightened action frees me from the errors of human judgment and causes me to know that I am an emanation of the One Life, that all beings are emanations of the One Life.*

*The true spiritual essence is all I know of each person. I think rightly and I love greatly. I love to let Love express through me.*

*I accept the fullness of life and am a distribution center of compassion, forgiveness, and love. I am blessed and prospered by Divine Love as it flows through me now.*

## Prayer of an Emissary of Peace

We pray because it is a natural flow of communication with the soul of our Soul—a flood of praise, gratitude, surrender, blessing, joy, longing—the full spectrum of expression. Prayer is the language of the heart.

The following prayer combines the personal and impersonal aspects of the Spirit. Again, please tailor the language to fit your own unique relationship with the God of your understanding.

*Right here and right now I recognize the God-Power, the God-Presence that is my very life, my very being. I am unified with this Presence. Something cries out from the depths of me: I am what Thou art, Thou art what I am.*

*With complete confidence I call forth the perfect peace that passeth human understanding. I know the people of all nations, the leaders of all nations are wrapped in that peace right now. I announce to all, "Peace, be still." The all-knowing Spirit is uplifting, healing and transforming the lives of all people and the leaders of all nations. This prayer is even now healing the global family, activating peace, loving kindness, unity.*

## *Meditation of an Emissary of Peace*

Buddhists, Christians, Hindus, religions of indigenous peoples—all have their techniques of meditation. An emissary of peace adopts meditation as a practice to experience the unbroken communion between the individual soul and the Over Soul. This oneness is the reality of our existence. The following is an example of a guided meditation on forgiveness.

To begin your practice, sit in a position of potency with your back straight yet relaxed. Keep your chest and heart area open and soft. If you are sitting on a chair, place your feet flat on the floor. Rest your hands on your thighs with your palms facing upwards in a mode of receptivity. Gently close your eyes and begin to breathe in a natural rhythm. As you become aware of your breath, know Infinite Life is breathing through you. As you feel your heartbeat, know the Cosmic Heart is beating as your own.

Mentally and emotionally accept for yourself and for all beings the compassion, mercy and unconditional love of Spirit. When you are ready, silently repeat to yourself the following:

*I am willing to heal those places within myself that are fearful, ashamed, unforgiving, or angry. Right now I make room in my heart for myself and all beings. We float in a sea of oneness. We are the "we" that is One.*

*I forgive myself for any ways in which I knowingly or unknowingly caused hurt or harm to any living being or creature. I forgive all who have ever hurt or harmed me. Everything between us is now cleared up. I am free and they are free, free in the freedom of our true nature.*

Continue following your breath in a natural rhythm as you embody the energy of the words you have been repeating. When your meditation time has ended close with a prayer in the language of your heart.

## *Forgiveness Exercises*

Forgiveness is essential in our journey to awakening and merits some further elaboration here. A working definition of forgiveness is: the conscious, intentional letting go of animosity, resentment, hate, blame, rancor or indifference to another or oneself. All forgiveness is, in actuality, self-forgiveness, because we are cleansing our own inner and outer household.

Forgiveness also frees us from self-abuse. What do I mean by this? When we harbor anger towards another individual an invisible signal is transmitted that draws into our magnetic field another person or circumstance that replays the same behaviors that triggered the original anger. Holding onto the anger continues a cycle of venting our anger, which is a form of self-abuse. It is vital to our well-being to release anger and make forgiveness a way of life.

You may practice the following forgiveness exercise at any time—during meditation, when doing affirmations, or simply by itself:

1. Write a statement of forgiveness on a sheet of paper or in your journal if you keep one. Prepare by reflecting on

individuals who have hurt you, whether in the present or those you haven't forgiven for hurts of the past. Include their names in your forgiveness statement. You needn't include all the details of the circumstances unless you feel doing so will support you in a healthy preparation for letting go. Here is an example:

*I forgive you, Jordan, for all the ways in which you have hurt me and our family over the years through your addiction. I send you thoughts of empowerment and I declare the truth that within you is all that you need reveal your wholeness. I see the highest and the best in you and trust that which seeks to emerge in, through and as your life. As I now replace my thoughts and feelings of negativity towards you with an energy of love and forgiveness, I know your spirit receives and responds to the loving energy of this prayer from my heart.*

2. If you have had or are in the midst of a circumstance where an individual who requires your forgiveness is not in your physical environment, you may use an affirmation such as the following:

*You have no power over me. Nothing you have said or done determines my happiness or success. I set myself free from any and all effects of your energy upon my life. I set you free with this act of forgiveness. I am free and you are free.*

3. In a situation where you want to be forgiven for some act of commission or omission and neither you or the person involved are prepared to have a face-to-face meeting, you may begin the forgiveness process within your own consciousness. (Since there is no distance between souls, this technique also works when the individual has died and made their transition into a new dimension of life.) This exercise is work you do within and upon *your own consciousness.* In other words, it is about *you,* not about convincing another person to act or be a certain way. It represents working with your mind to loosen up and release judgment and replace it with forgiveness, compassion, and right action.

*As I sit in the energy of our relationship, I ask your forgiveness for any hurt or harm I have knowingly or unknowingly caused you. A healing of the heart and spirit has now begun between us in the depth of our true nature as love, compassion and forgiveness. You are free and I am free. All is well between us.*

## *About the Author*

Michael Bernard Beckwith is the visionary founder and spiritual director of the Agape International Spiritual Center located in Los Angeles, California. The Agape Movement has a local membership of thousands, and hundreds-of-thousands of affiliates worldwide.

Agape is the outgrowth of Dr. Beckwith's many years of explorations in consciousness. As a freshman student at Morehouse College in Atlanta, Georgia, Michael was exposed to the Christian mysticism of the renowned philosopher and humanitarian Dr. Howard Thurman. Insightful glimpses into the spiritual realm familiar to him since childhood were given credence and encouragement to flourish.

By the time Michael transferred to the University of Southern California, he had begun to experience conscious jolts of spiritual awakening. Led to discard a traditional college curriculum, he entered a period of intense study of Eastern and Western spirituality which culminated in his enrollment in the Ernest Holmes College of Ministry, founded by the late Dr. Ernest

Holmes. Beckwith's soul-life married East and West, which today is one of the distinguishing hallmarks of his unique trans-denominational spiritual center.

In 1986, Dr. Beckwith's inner vision revealed a world united on an ethical basis of humankind's highest evolutionary development spiritually, educationally, culturally, philanthropically, and socially. Applying the Life Visioning Process (LVP) originated by Dr. Beckwith, committed associates came forward to participate in his vision, resulting in the formation of the Agape spiritual community. Agape's local humanitarian programs feed the homeless, serve prisoners and their families, provide hospice and grief support, and advocate the preservation of the planet's environmental resources. Its international programs feed, house, and educate children whose lives have been ravaged by wars, AIDS, and natural disasters, and assist in the rebuilding of communities with schools, orphanages, libraries, hospitals and clinics.

Dr. Beckwith serves as national co-director of A Season for Nonviolence, an international movement co-founded in partnership with Arun Gandhi, grandson of Mahatma K. Gandhi and founder of the M.K. Gandhi Institute for

Nonviolence. SNV promotes and teaches the principles of ahimsa—nonviolence—practiced by Mahatma Gandhi and Dr. Martin Luther King, Jr. He is a founding member of the Association for Global New Thought, convener of The Synthesis Dialogues with His Holiness the Dalai Lama of Tibet.

Thousands gather at Agape on Sundays and Wednesdays to learn from Dr. Beckwith's connection to the timeless realm as he teaches timely truths applicable to the challenges of twenty-first-century living. His is a passionately unique voice, announcing to all that they are an intentional, vital, and beloved presence in the universe.

Dr. Beckwith is a featured teacher in the book and film *The Secret*. He has appeared on the Oprah Winfrey Show, and Larry King Live. He is author of the award winning book *Spiritual Liberation~Fulfilling Your Soul's Potential, The Answer Is You, Inspirations of the Heart, 40 Day Mind Fast Soul Feast,* and *A Manifesto of Peace.*

## *A Personal Word About Pure Synergy,™ My PBS Special Sponsor...*

When I travel throughout the United States and abroad speaking and conducting seminars, I always enjoy that part of the event when I get to dialogue with the participants. Without exception, in addition to their questions on spiritual matters, the next most frequent one is, "What's the secret to your energy and stamina to do all that you do?" When I respond, "One of my secrets is Pure Synergy," they at first think I'm using a spiritual euphemism for energy. The truth is, "energy" is a perfect synonym for Pure Synergy™, because that's one of the utmost benefits I receive from its use.

I have personally known Mitchell May, the founder of The Synergy Company and maker of Pure Synergy™, for many years. My wife and I have toured his production facilities during our many visits to Utah and always leave deeply impressed with Mitchell's dedication to the purest processing methods that retain the life force of his products.

Pure Synergy is what I use daily in the green drink I prepare for myself and my family. After much experimentation, I have conclusive evidence that its organic and kosher ingredients provide the ultimate combination of nutrients, vitamins and minerals that are most easily digested and utilized by the human body. Mitchell's life-threatening accident that led him to create and produce Pure Synergy™ is not only inspiring, it birthed his commitment to offering the world a product with extraordinary healing and life-enhancing properties.

I wholeheartedly recommend Pure Synergy™ to everyone who wants to have the holistic benefits of vibrant health and vitality.

*Michael B. Beckwith*

For more information, go to:
**www.TheSynergyCompany.com**
Or Call 1-800-723-0277
Please tell them I sent you.

# *Other Offerings to Enrich Your Life from Agape Media International*

Michael Bernard Beckwith, founder and spiritual director of the Agape International Spiritual Center in Los Angeles, launched Agape Media International (AMI) as an innovative company dedicated to promoting artists and art forms that uplift the human spirit and inspire individuals to contribute their own talents to the creation of a world that works for everyone.

The French word "ami" means "beloved friend," and AMI's purpose is to be just that as a vehicle within the global Agape movement that produces, promotes and distributes films, books, music, online media and television programs that spread the message of Agape—unconditional love—worldwide.

## Books by Michael Bernard Beckwith

*The Answer Is You*
*Spiritual Liberation - Fulfilling Your Soul's Potential*
*40-Day Mind Fast Soul Feast*

*Living from the Overflow*
*Inspirations of the Heart*
*A Manifesto of Peace*

## Audio Programs by Michael Bernard Beckwith

The Life Visioning Process (6-CDs)

Life Visioning (2-CDs)

Life Visioning Kit (2 CDs, 30 Cards,
   45-page workbook)

The Rhythm of a Descended Master (4-CDs)

Your Soul's Evolution

## DVDs

The Answer Is You, Deluxe Edition DVD

Spiritual Liberation, the Movie

Living in the Revelation • Michael Bernard Beckwith
   with Rickie Byars Beckwith & the Agape
   International Choir

Revelation 8 – Quantum Quickening (series of 8 DVDs)
   • Michael Bernard Beckwith • Dr. David R. Hawkins
   • Bishop Carlton Pearson • Venerable Dhyani Ywahoo

• Dr. Sue Morter • Rickie Byars Beckwith •
Rev. Shiela McKeithen • Mystical, Magical, Moving
Spiritual Theatre • The Wisdom Gathering

**Music CDs**

Music from the PBS Special – The Answer Is You
Siedah Garrett, Will.I.Am, Niki Haris, Rickie Byars
Beckwith, the Agape International Choir

Jami Lula & Spirit In The House / *There's A Healin'
Goin' On*

Charles Holt / *I Am*

Rickie Byars Beckwith / *Supreme Inspiration*

Ester Nicholson / *Child Above the Sun*

Ben Dowling / *Pathways of Peace*

Michael Bernard Beckwith / *Energetic Shapeshifter*

**Inspirational Cards**

Life Lift-Off Cards • Michael Bernard Beckwith

www.agapemedia-international.com

# *Notes*

# *Notes*

# *Notes*

## *Notes*